A M A Z I N G
SEA
FACTS

Su Swallow
Illustrated by Polly Raynes
Consultant: Dr Tony Rice
Editor: Anne Civardi
Designed by Jane Warring

Contents

MALLARD
PRESS

An imprint of BDD Promotional Book Company, Inc., 666 Fifth Avenue, New York, N.Y. 10103

Life in the Sea

The deep, dark and stormy oceans of the world are teeming with life, from tiny plants and animals much smaller than a pin head to the great blue whale. Clever mammals, strange worms, shellfish, jellyfish, corals and starfish all make their homes under the water.

The most varied group of animals in the sea are the fish. There are round fish and flat fish, fish that can walk or fly, and fish that can breathe out of water. They live everywhere, from the sunlit surface to the blackest sea bed.

A Fishy Tale

There are about 12,000 different kinds of fish. The biggest of all is the gigantic whale shark which can grow up to 45 ft (15 m) long. The tiny dwarf pygmy goby, only 0.3 in (7.5 mm) long, is the smallest fish in the world.

All fish are vertebrates which means that they have backbones. Most have a bony skeleton but sharks, rays and skates have a skeleton made of very hard cartilage, or gristle.

Fish do not have lungs. They use their gills to take in oxygen from the water. Water goes in through their mouths and over their gills, where the oxygen is absorbed into the bloodstream.

A fish uses its pairs of fins to help steer its streamlined body through the water. The single fins on its belly and back are for balance. The tail fins help to push the fish forwards.

Most fish have round, overlapping scales. Shark scales are like small, pointed teeth, which makes their skin rough. Fish that do not have any scales have thick, tough skin.

Fish cannot close their eyes because they have no eyelids. But they do sleep, some lying quite still on the sea bed.

Some fish have bright markings, with spots and stripes of every color. Others are dark and dull.

Safety in Numbers

Some fish, such as herrings, swim about in huge shoals. A predator faced with thousands of prey can become confused and fail to catch a single one.

All Change!

Most wrasses are very brightly colored. They may change color in the breeding season or as they get older. Some change sex when they are a few years old. They may even change back again before they die.

Pipes and Pouches

Female banded pipefish lay their eggs in a pouch on the male's long, thin body.

A few weeks later, when the eggs have hatched, the pouch opens and the young fish swim away.

A fish's color may help it to hide from or confuse its enemies, defend itself, find a mate, or signal that it owns a particular territory.

A line of sensitive hairs, called the lateral line, runs down either side of a fish's body. The hairs, which lie in jelly under the skin, pick up vibrations in the water caused by currents or other sea creatures.

Sea Facts

The oceans cover almost 3/4 of the surface of the Earth. There are three great oceans – the Pacific, Atlantic and Indian Oceans. The biggest and deepest is the Pacific Ocean which covers almost 1/3 of the Earth's surface.

The deepest spot in the ocean is about 36,089 ft (11,000 m) deep.

Even in the hottest parts of the world, the water deeper than a few hundred yards is no warmer than 37°F (3°C).

Seawater contains lots of salt. There is enough salt in the sea to cover the land with a layer over 330 ft (100 m) thick. The Red Sea has the saltiest water.

On the Seashore

Life on the seashore is not easy for the creatures that live there. As the tide moves in and out, most beaches are covered by salt water and then exposed to the air. Seashore animals have to stop themselves from drying out and protect themselves from the waves that crash on to the shore.

On sandy and muddy shores, many creatures burrow to keep damp and hide from their enemies. On rocky shores, shellfish and other animals cling on to the rocks so tightly that it is almost impossible to dislodge them. But on pebbly beaches, few creatures can survive among the shifting stones.

The High Life

As the tide comes in, the seashore comes to life. Seaweed that has been lying flat at low tide floats upright, and hundreds of sea creatures begin to move about in search of food.

A Spiny Disguise

The spiny spider crab is not easy to spot. It collects small pieces of seaweed or sponge with its claws and fixes them on to spines and bristles all over its shell until it is camouflaged.

Barnacles, up to 30,000 per 3 sq ft (1 sq m), open their shells under the water and push out feathery tentacles. The tentacles catch plankton to eat, moving in and out of the shell about twice every second.

Somersaulting Starfish

If the common starfish is accidentally turned on to its back, it rights itself by turning a complete somersault. First it slowly lifts up the tip of one arm until it can grip a rocky surface with the suckers on its arm. Then it folds itself in half and pulls on three other arms until it is the right way up again.

Did You Know?

There are over 1,000,000 miles (1,600,000 km) of coastline around the continents and islands of the world.

Some sandy beaches are black because they are formed from volcanic lava.

Hermit crabs do not have shells of their own. Instead they live in the empty shells of dead sea animals. As the crabs grow, they find bigger shells to move into.

The tides are caused by the pull of gravity from the Moon and the Sun. Twice a day, they make the level of the sea rise and fall.

One kind of razor shell can burrow into the sand so fast that it is almost impossible to dig it out whole.

Limpets move about under the water to feed on algae. As the tide goes out, they always return to exactly the same spot. They scrape out small hollows in the rocks which match the shape of their shells perfectly.

At low tide, the beadlet sea anemone looks like a blob of jelly. When it is covered with water, it puts out 200 tentacles to trap its food.

Buried in a Burrow

The king rag worm hides itself in a burrow in the sand, leaving no trace of its huge size on the surface. It can grow over 3 ft (1 m) long and has powerful jaws for attacking other worms.

Tread Carefully!

Weever fish lie buried in the sand in shallow water waiting for shrimps and other food to pass by. If the spines behind a weever's head are touched, they shoot out a powerful poison.

Every day, mussels pump up to 37 gallons (140 litres) of water through their bodies to feed on the plankton it contains.

Cities of Coral

Huge "cities" of coral grow in the warm, shallow waters around tropical coastlines. These beautiful and brilliantly colored coral reefs are the largest living structures on Earth. They provide hunting grounds and hiding places for all kinds of strange sea creatures.

The thousands of tiny animals that build the reefs are called polyps. A polyp has a soft body which is protected by a hard outer skeleton of limestone. The coral grows when the animals send out branch-like buds. In each bud there is an animal with its own tiny skeleton.

Record-breakers of the Reef

Animals that live on coral reefs are often bigger and brighter than the creatures that live in other parts of the sea.

Huge sea slugs, up to 1 ft (30 cm) long, live on coral reefs. They feed on sea anemones. The poison from the anemones goes into their own skin and protects them.

Many coral reef fish have bright markings, with spots and stripes of every color. The strong colors make them almost invisible against the colors of the reef and help to camouflage them from predators.

Coral Eaters

The crown-of-thorns starfish feeds on coral. In a day it can destroy an area of reef that would have taken 100 years to grow, about 3.3 ft (1 m) square.

This starfish is eaten by triton snails. Where the snails have been collected for their shells, the starfish have destroyed huge areas of reef.

Thousands of brightly colored sea anemones live on coral reefs.

Parasite Pickers

Some large fish allow tiny fish to pick the parasites off their bodies, and even from inside their mouths. They often line up for this service at cleaning stations on the reef, where the cleaner fish dance about in the water to attract customers.

Moray eels, the largest of all eels, lurk in dark corners during the day and prey on shrimps, crabs, fish and even octopuses at night. Some moray eels may grow over 10 ft (3 m) long.

Close Encounters

Clown fish can swim safely among the poisonous tentacles of a sea anemone by covering themselves with slime. The sea anemones feed on bits of food left over by the clown fish.

Did You Know?

The Great Barrier Reef, off the east coast of Australia, is the largest reef in the world. It is over 1,090 miles (1,750 km) long and has more than 400 different types of coral.

Tiny algae live inside coral polyps. These plants use the Sun's energy to make oxygen and sugar. They help the coral to build the reefs.

The female of one small crab spends its whole life trapped inside a coral gall, which grows around the crab. Food and water wash in through tiny holes in the coral.

A pearlfish spends most of its life inside a sea cucumber. It comes out from the end of the cucumber to feed at night. It may also eat the sea cucumber's internal organs which quickly grow again.

Shrimpfish hide from their enemies, head down, among the prickly spines of sea urchins. Cardinal fish also take cover among the spines and clean the urchin's body.

The giant clam, which lives in the Indo-Pacific Ocean, is the largest clam in the world. It feeds on plankton, and has a shell which can be over 3.3 ft (1 m) wide.

7

Fantastic Feeders

Some sea creatures feed every day in order to survive. Others manage on an occasional huge meal. Animals that cannot move about have to wait for food to come within their reach. Those that can swim may cross great oceans to seek their prey. Many sea creatures have some very strange ways of finding and catching their food.

Strange Stomachs

Starfish smell out oysters, mussels and scallops to eat. They wrap their stomachs over the shellfish and digest it before pulling their stomachs back in.

A starfish uses tiny suckers on its arms to pry open the shells of a mussel. Then it squeezes its stomach through the gap to eat the mussel's flesh.

Hitching a Ride

A strange type of perch, called a remora, attaches itself to larger sea creatures, especially sharks, turtles, whales and porpoises, by a sucker on top of its head.

Once it has hitched a ride to a good feeding area, it leaves its "host" to search for food. Remoras also feed on the leftovers of their host's meals.

Sounding Them Out

Dolphins need to eat up to $1/10$ of their body weight in fish every day. They hunt in herds, working together to round up shoals of herring, sardines and other fish.

To find their prey they use echo-location. The sounds they make send back echoes when they hit a shoal of fish and tell the dolphins where to find the fish.

Blowing Bubbles

The humpback whale traps fish to eat. It swims underneath them and blows a stream of bubbles from its blowhole. The fish stay inside the circle of bubbles, and the whale swims up to swallow them.

A Clean Sweep

Up to 3,000 thin tellins live together in 10 sq ft (1 sq m) of sand. They each have two long siphons which they use to suck up food, like a vacuum cleaner, from the sea floor. Sometimes fish eat the thin tellins' siphons.

Dolphins are one of the most intelligent animals in the world. They have been trained by the US Navy as underwater guards and for other secret work.

Underwater Weeds

All animals that live in the sea depend on plants for survival. They either eat the plants or feed on other plant-eating animals. Seaweeds, sea grasses and the microscopic plants in plankton are the plants of the sea. They can only grow in shallow water because they need sunlight to make their food. There are no plants in the dark waters of the deep ocean.

Clusters of "flowers" on kelp fronds are not really flowers at all. They are lots of tiny animals with poisonous tentacles.

King of the Seaweeds

Huge forests of kelp, a large brown seaweed, grow along many rocky shores, below the surface of the sea. Some giant kelps can grow 3.3 ft (1 m) a day, until they are over 330 ft (100 m) long.

Kelp and other seaweeds do not have any roots. They grip on to rocks with finger-like strands, called holdfasts, which grow at the end of the fronds. Many shrimps, crabs, fish, sea urchins and other sea animals live in the holdfasts.

Sea urchins feed on seaweed, which they scrape off rocks with their five teeth. Plagues of sea urchins can destroy whole forests of kelp.

Cows in the Meadow

Sea cows, or manatees, are huge, slow and heavy mammals which live in warm, tropical waters. They graze on sea grasses which spread out like underwater fields along some coasts.

All Wrapped Up

A Californian sea otter wraps itself up in strands of kelp before it settles down for the night. The strong seaweed stops the animal from drifting away while it rests or sleeps.

Monkey Tricks

A sea horse is not a good swimmer. It hangs on to seaweed with its tail. An Australian sea horse has leafy flaps of skin to help it hide among the seaweed.

Did You Know?

The Sargasso Sea, in the North Atlantic, is named after the Sargassum seaweed which grows there in huge quantities and floats on the surface.

Red seaweeds can grow in deeper, darker water than brown seaweeds. This is because they are more efficient at using any available light.

People in Japan and China grow seaweeds on farms in the sea. They eat the seaweed raw or cook it as a vegetable.

Billions of tiny sea plants use sunlight to make oxygen. Scientists think they produce 70% of all the oxygen breathed by living things on Earth.

Salty Tears

The only iguanas that live in the sea are found on the Galapagos Islands. They feed on seaweed. As they eat, they swallow a lot of salt water. The salt comes out through their tear glands.

11

Escape or Die

It is not easy for mammals and fish to survive in the vast open sea. Deep down in the water, there is no seaweed to hide in, no sand to burrow in and often no rocks to hide behind. The creatures that live there have developed some amazing tricks to stay alive and to escape from their enemies.

All Puffed Up

Puffer fish can make themselves too big for their enemies to swallow by filling themselves up with water. If they are pulled up in a fishing net, they blow up with air, just like a big prickly soccer ball.

Taking Flight

Flying fish leap high out of the water to escape from fish that are chasing them. Their tail fins, which act like propellers, beat from side to side until the fish take off at speeds of over 37 mph (60 km/h).

Their wings are really big fins which spread out wide to help them glide through the air. The fish do not beat them as they fly.

Four-winged flying fish can glide further than those with only two wings. They can travel about 164 ft (50 m) in each glide.

Bodyguard Aboard

Some hermit crabs put a sea anemone on their shell. The stinging tentacles of the anemone help to protect the crab. The anemone feeds on food scraps left by the crab.

Poisonous Cucumbers

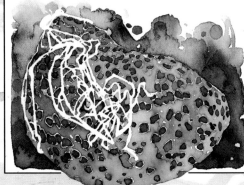

Sea cucumbers shoot out a mass of sticky, poisonous threads from their mouths to frighten off a hungry fish. Some also shoot out bits of their insides which quickly grow again.

These strange creatures have sticky tentacles around their mouths to pick up their food.

Shock Tactics

Electric rays can produce up to 200 volts of electricity to stun an attacker. Long ago, electric shocks from these fish were used by the Romans to cure gout, a disease of the joints.

Often, flying fish escape one enemy, only to be caught by another. Boobies and other sea birds grab the fish before they dive back into the water.

The wind may lift a flying fish high into the air. Some have landed on the decks of big ships.

The fish dip down several times during a flight. They take off again by swishing their tails in the water.

Did You Know?

To escape an attacker, cuttlefish, octopuses and squid shoot out a dark ink which acts as a smoke screen. Sometimes the ink is luminous and dazzles the enemy.

One puffer fish, which the Japanese like to eat, has some very poisonous parts. Many people die each year from eating the fish.

Crabs and lobsters can shed some of their limbs to stop themselves being eaten. In time the limbs grow again.

Many fish can change color to keep safe. Tropical grouper fish can develop spots and stripes in an instant.

If a starfish's arms are damaged, it can cast them off and grow new ones. It can grow up to four from one remaining arm.

On the March

Once a year, thousands of spiny lobsters set off along the sea floor to search for food in deeper waters. To keep safe, and to protect each other from any enemies, they march in single file in a long line of about 50, touching each other with their antennae. Their long journey may take up to a month.

Carried Away

Many sea creatures, from tiny zooplankton to huge jellyfish, are carried long distances by the strong ocean currents. Some spend their whole lives drifting about on the surface of the sea or just below it. Others are moved by the currents and tides to speed them on their way to and from their spawning grounds.

A Man-of-War

The Portuguese man-of-war does not have many enemies but sometimes sea turtles attack and eat it. Its deadly stinging tentacles can paralyze and kill a fish instantly. The poison is also very painful to human beings.

The tentacles, which can be over 66 ft (20 m) long, are covered with poisonous spines which shoot into a victim when they are touched.

All Washed Up

In the Spring, huge numbers of grunion swim with the rising tide up on to some Californian beaches. There the females lay their eggs. The next high tide washes the eggs back out to sea, just as they are ready to hatch.

Tiny nomeid fish are not hurt by the jellyfish's tentacles and often swim among them to hide from bigger fish.

The float acts as a sail which catches the wind as the man-of-war bobs about on the water.

Unlike other types of jellyfish, the man-of-war is not just one animal but a drifting colony of hundreds of tiny animals. These animals have different jobs to do, from catching prey to having babies.

Did You Know?

Plankton comes from the Greek word which means "wandering". This describes the way plankton drifts about on the water.

Sometimes some types of plant plankton suddenly grow very fast, turning the sea red. These "red tides" are poisonous and can kill millions of fish, sea birds and other sea creatures.

Currents used to be traced by dropping bottles into the sea. When the bottles were found, the places were marked on a map to follow the currents.

Huge tides happen in the Bay of Fundy, in Canada. Here the highest tides are more than 50 ft (15 m) above the low tide mark.

A Deadly Dose

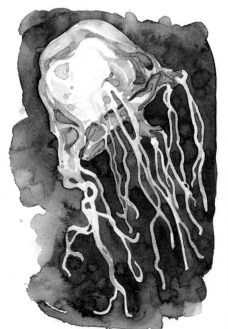

One sting from a sea wasp, which lives off the coast of Australia, can kill a person in a minute. More than 60 people have died from sea wasp stings in the past 100 years.

Taken for a Ride

European eels are born in the Sargasso Sea and then carried thousands of miles by the currents of the Gulf Stream.

The tiny larvae cross the Atlantic Ocean to river mouths where they move upstream for their adult life. Years later, they return to the Sargasso Sea to spawn and die.

Catching the Tide

Horseshoe crabs crawl ashore to spawn in early Summer. The female lays thousands of eggs in the sand, out of reach of all but the highest tides. The next very high tide uncovers the eggs, just as the larvae are ready to hatch and head for the sea.

In Deep Water

There is not enough sunlight in the sea for plants to grow below about 400 ft (120 m). But some of the most fantastic sea creatures of all live in water up to 40 times as deep. Although they live in the coldest, darkest parts of the seas and oceans, where food is hard to find, many grow to be much larger than related species living in shallow waters.

Lights in the Dark

Nearly all deep-sea creatures are cold-blooded and have body temperatures close to the chilly temperature of the water. Most of the fish that live below about 1,000 ft (300 m) have lights on their strange-looking bodies. In some species, the light is produced by bacteria that live in certain parts of the fish's body. Other fish have their own light-making cells.

Coming Back to Life

In 1938, fishermen in the Indian Ocean caught a strange-looking blue fish about 6.6 ft (2 m) long. It was a coelacanth. Until then, scientists thought that it had been extinct for millions of years. This odd fish has big, thick scales covering its strong body, and gives birth to live babies.

At Arm's Length

Giant squid are the largest invertebrates, animals without a backbone, in the world and can grow up to 66 ft (20 m) long. They have ten arms, which are covered in suckers, for holding on to their prey. They have the biggest eyes of any animal.

A Clever Shell

A nautilus has a beautiful shell which is divided into 30 separate chambers filled with gas. It can sink, rise and swim by changing the amount of gas in the chambers. Nautiluses usually live in very deep water during the daytime. At night they come close to the surface to feed.

Greedy Gulpers

Gulpers make sure they have enough food by being able to eat prey that is even bigger than themselves. They have enormous jaws and their stomachs stretch so that they can swallow their victims whole.

Did You Know?

The colors in sunlight are absorbed at different depths as they pass through the water. Red disappears first, then yellow and then green and blue. This is why brightly-colored fish look black in deep water.

There are about 600 species of sea spider, which have up to 12 legs. The largest live in very deep water. Sea spiders are not related to land spiders. They are not really spiders at all.

Some deep-sea prawns are bright red so that their enemies cannot see them in the water. Some deep-sea shrimps and squids can shoot out a luminous ink to warn away predators.

Lobsters can live for 50 years and weigh up to 44 lb (20 kg).

The pattern of lights varies from one species of deep-sea fish to another so that the fish can recognize their own species to mate with. The lights also help some fish to see or attract their prey in the dark water.

Giants of the Ocean

Whales are the largest creatures in the world. They are warm-blooded mammals and give birth to live babies which they feed with their milk. Although they come up to breathe, whales can stay underwater for up to an hour by storing oxygen in their blood and muscles as well as their lungs.

Baleen whales, including the giant blue whale, feed on tiny shrimp-like animals, called krill. A fringe of bony plates in the whale's mouth sieves the food out of the water. Toothed whales feed on fish, squid and even seals. They grasp their prey in their teeth and then swallow it whole.

Biggest of All

The blue whale is the biggest animal that has ever lived. It can grow over 100 ft (30 m) long, much longer than any dinosaur.

Long Distance Swimmer

In short bursts, these whales can swim up to 19 mph (30 km/h). The fastest whales can swim twice as fast, powered only by their tails.

Every year, gray whales set off on the longest migration journey of any mammal. They move from their feeding grounds in the Arctic to breed off the coast of California.

By the time they return, when their calves are only two months old, they have swum about 13,000 miles (20,000 km).

Deep Sea Diver

A great sperm whale may dive down 3,300 ft (1,000 m) in search of a giant squid to eat. The squid's tentacles leave huge sucker marks on the whale's head.

Long in the Tooth

The male narwhal's tusk is really a giant tooth. One of his two teeth keeps growing.

It pierces through the narwhal's top lip. The longest tusk ever seen was nearly 10 ft (3 m) long.

Baby whales, called calves, are born under the water, tail first. As soon as the head appears, the mother pushes the calf up to the surface to take its first breath.

A blue whale calf weighs about 2 tons when it is born. It drinks 158 gallons (600 litres) of milk a day, and may double its weight in a week. At seven months it weighs 23 tons, as much as four African elephants.

Tasty Tongues

Killer whales sometimes attack baleen whales for food. They only eat the whale's tongue, which may weigh as much as an elephant. They leave the rest of the body for hungry scavengers.

Did You Know?

Whales make different sounds to communicate with each other. They moan and whistle and make clicking sounds, and even sing complicated "songs".

Scientists find out how old a toothed whale is by counting the yearly growth rings in a slice from one of its teeth.

The largest animal in the world feeds on some of the smallest creatures in the sea. In one day, a blue whale may swallow up to 4 million krill.

If a whale gets stranded on a beach, its distress call attracts other whales of the same species. They, in turn, may become stranded and their calls attract more whales. Herds of great sperm whales are often stranded in this way.

Whales are shaped like fish but their tails move up and down when they swim instead of from side to side. Sometimes, they slap the water with their huge tails, just before diving. The noise can be heard several miles away.

The Dark Sea Bed

If you could explore the floor of the sea, you would cross great plains, climb ridges and high mountains and look down into deep, dark trenches. Parts of the sea floor are more than 6 miles (10 km) below the surface.

Many of the strange creatures that live at the bottom of the world's seas and oceans survive by feeding on dead plants and animals. These dead animals fall down on them from the busy ocean layers far above.

Once in a Lifetime

Octopuses live by themselves on the sea floor, in shallow or deep water. By day, they hide away among rocks or in holes. At night, they hunt for shellfish to eat.

The female lays eggs only once in her lifetime. After mating, she moves into a cave, where she lays thousands of eggs. For several weeks she looks after them until they hatch, and then she dies.

An octopus can jet-propel itself away from predators. It can also squeeze through tiny gaps, change the color and texture of its skin to match its background, and shoot out a cloud of black ink to confuse an enemy.

Newly-hatched octopuses are tiny. They float on the top of the water as part of the plankton. When they are about $1/2$ in (1 cm) long, they settle on the sea bed.

Animals of a Feather

The sea pen, like coral, is made up of many tiny animals living together. They form a feathery shape, on a long stalk. Some of the largest sea pens live in very deep water.

In 1960, the bathyscaphe Trieste, with its two-man crew, dived down nearly 36,000 ft (11,000 m) to the sea bed. It took almost five hours to get to the bottom and is the deepest anyone has ever been.

The mud on the ocean floor is called ooze and may be hundreds, even thousands, of feet thick. It contains the skeletons of plants and animals that have died and sunk to the bottom.

Underwater earthquakes and volcanic eruptions can cause huge waves, called tsunamis, to form on the surface of the sea. They can also start great avalanches of sand and mud under the sea.

Octopuses have excellent eyesight. Their eyes always stay level, whatever the angle of their bodies.

Hugging the Hot Spots

Strange life forms cluster around hot springs that rise from the sea bed. The water, heated by lava inside the Earth to temperatures up to 752°F (400°C), rushes up through cracks in the rock.

Giant tube worms, up to 9 ft (3 m) long, live around the hot springs. They have no mouths or digestive systems, but absorb wastes from bacteria living inside them. The springs also attract blind shrimps that have heat sensors to guide them.

Starry Sea Floor

Brittle stars are common on the sea floor. They have five thin arms that are easily broken, but can grow again. Some burrow into the mud, leaving only the tips of their arms visible.

Sea Legs

The tripod fish props itself up on the sea floor on three "legs" which are really stiff threads that stick out from three fins. These "legs" stop the fish from sinking into the soft mud.

21

Turtle Territory

Sea snakes are one of the largest groups of reptiles in the world. They live in warm, tropical waters, feeding on fish. Many are deadly poisonous and have brightly colored bodies to warn off any predators.

Sea turtles also live in tropical waters. They move clumsily on land but are excellent swimmers. The fastest reptile in water is the Pacific leatherback turtle, which can swim at over 19 mph (30 km/h).

Beach Party

The only time that sea turtles leave the water is when the females go ashore to lay their eggs. Males may never return to land after hatching.

The turtles return to the same breeding places, called rookeries, each year. They may even use the very beach on which they hatched.

Vegetarian Turtles

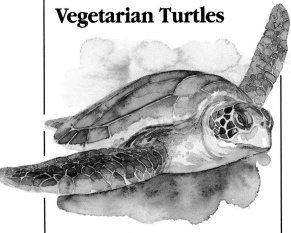

Most turtles eat shellfish, jellyfish and other meat, as well as some plants. But green turtles mostly eat green plants. They are probably named after the green fat in their bodies, rather than their diet or color.

The Call of the Sea

When baby sea turtles hatch, they always head for the water, even if their nest is out of sight of the sea. But it is a very dangerous journey. As many as half of them may be snatched up and eaten by hungry shore birds.

Big and Fierce

Saltwater crocodiles, which grow up to 20 ft (6 m) long, are the largest reptiles in the world. They live along coasts from India to Australia.

When it catches a large animal, the crocodile turns over and over in the water, drowning its prey. Then it bites it up into small pieces with its razor-sharp teeth.

No one yet knows for sure how turtles find their way to their rookeries. But some scientists think they may navigate by the Sun and stars. Others think the turtles use smell to find their way.

All the turtle eggs laid in different nests in a rookery will hatch at about the same time.

Did You Know?

A green turtle travels further than other sea turtles. To reach the beaches where it lays its eggs, it sometimes swims more than 1,400 miles (2,200 km).

A leatherback turtle, which has a leathery skin over its shell, is the largest sea turtle of all. It can grow over 6.6 ft (2 m) long and weigh 1,100 lb (500 kg). The heaviest leatherback weighed almost double that, about the same as 10 large men.

The most poisonous snake in the world is a sea snake which lives off the northwest coast of Australia.

Slippery Customer

Some sea snakes lay their eggs on the beach, but most give birth to live young in the water. They have flattened bodies for swimming, and can spend up to three hours under the water before coming up for air.

Most of these snakes swim alone. But sometimes large groups of yellow-bellied sea snakes can be seen drifting together on bundles of weeds and sticks. These drift lines attract lots of fish for the snakes to eat.

Oceans of Ice

Some warm-blooded animals that live in the Arctic and the Antarctic spend most of their time in the freezing water. They come out on to the ice to give birth and to rear their babies, and to rest. These animals often travel vast distances over the ice and through the water.

Waddling About

Penguins have wings but they cannot fly. In the water, they can swim very fast, using their short wings like flippers. On land, they waddle and hop about on their stubby legs, or slide down icy slopes on their stomachs.

Emperor penguins, the largest penguins in the world, are about 3 ft (1 m) tall. They can dive at least 660 ft (200 m), deeper than any other bird.

After the female emperor has laid her egg she goes back to the sea to find food. Standing on the cold ice for two months, the male carries the egg on his feet, keeping it warm under a special flap of skin.

A Shouting Match

Seals move on to the ice in the breeding season. Male elephant seals defend their territory by roaring at possible rivals.

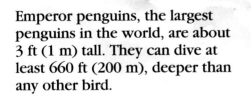

They inflate their huges noses to roar even louder. Often the seals fight each other fiercely.

The Greenhouse Effect!

The hairs of a polar bear's fur are hollow and transparent. They allow heat through to the bear's skin and trap it in the same way as the glass on a greenhouse traps heat. The bear's skin is black, so it absorbs heat well.

Polar bears are excellent swimmers and sometimes swim hundreds of miles out to sea. But their fur does not keep them warm in the water. Instead, a thick layer of fat insulates them against the freezing cold.

Did You Know?

A hooded seal feeds its pup with milk for only four days, the shortest time that any mammal gives milk to its young.

Polar bears can walk silently across the ice because they have thick patches of fur between their paw pads to muffle the sound.

Walruses have throat pouches which they can inflate with air to hold them up in the water as they sleep. Their tusks are long teeth.

Although seals live in the sea, they sometimes swim up rivers and surprise people inland.

Polar bears know which holes to watch in the ice when they are waiting to catch a seal. They can smell where the seal has been because it leaves behind a strong scent. Once a seal pokes its head through a hole, the polar bear kills it with its huge paw. One blow can kill a seal weighing 800 lbs (350 kg).

A penguin resting on an ice floe may end up as a meal for a killer whale. Whales sometimes work together to tip up the ice so that the penguin slides into one of their huge open mouths.

Lurking Low

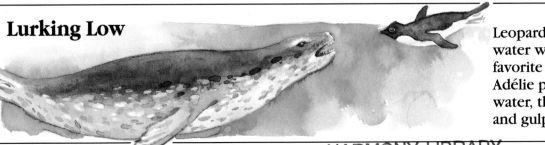

Leopard seals lurk under the water waiting to catch their favorite food. As soon as an Adélie penguin jumps into the water, the seal grabs it head-first and gulps it down its throat.

Life on the Edge

All kinds of strange sea creatures live near the coast in river mouths, where the salt water of the sea meets fresh river water. Waders and seashore birds flock to estuaries, mudflats and saltmarshes to feed on shellfish, crabs, marine worms and other sea creatures. Some of these animals have to survive not only the rising and falling tides, but also changes in the saltiness of the water.

Fighting Fiddlers

At low tide, groups of fiddler crabs can be seen scuttling across a saltmarsh. The male has an extra-large, brightly colored right claw which it uses to fight off other males and to attract females to its burrow.

Target Practice

The fish squirts a jet of water out of its mouth up to its vicitim. As soon as the insect drops, the fish snaps it up and eats it. But most of the time, archerfish feed on prey swimming in the water.

When they are very hungry, archerfish leap out of the mangrove swamps to catch their prey. They can also shoot down an insect that may be 3 ft (1 m) or more above the water.

Did You Know?

Gray mullet move into river mouths to feed. They suck up mud to find worms and algae.

Ghost shrimps live in sandy burrows with small clams, tiny crabs and little goby fish to keep them company.

Mangrove crabs climb up mangrove trees and eat the leaves. They also spend a lot of time in burrows in the mud.

The sea lamprey has no jaw. It clamps on to other fish with its round sucker mouth and rasps away at the flesh of its prey with a toothed tongue. The sea lamprey moves up estuaries to spawn in fresh water.

Skipping Across the Mud

Mangrove trees grow in saltmarshes, estuaries and big muddy swamps in the warm waters of the tropics. Their long, tangled roots make a safe hide-out for small sea creatures.

Floundering Flatfish

Like other flatfish, a flounder has both eyes on one side of its body. Soon after hatching, its round body becomes flat and one eye moves next to the other. The fish then settles on the sea bed on the side without eyes.

Lightning Strike

A mantis shrimp stabs its prey with its large front legs, which give the shrimp its name. It strikes at about 4/1,000 of a second with its claw-like leg. This is one of the fastest animal movements known.

Strange fish called mudskippers live in the muddy mangrove swamps of Southeast Asia. At low tide, they skip over the mud, using their short, thick fins. They climb on to rocks, muddy beaches and even trees.

Mudskippers spend much of their time out of the water. Like frogs, they can breathe partly through their skin. They also take in oxygen from water trapped in their gills.

Deadly Weapons

Tales of ships and sailors overpowered by huge sea monsters may not be true, but some of the animals in the sea are very dangerous. The most deadly are not necessarily the biggest. The biggest shark, the largest whale and the giant octopus are all gentle giants that do not attack people or treat them as their enemies.

Coral Cruiser

Many fish are armed with poisonous spines to defend themselves against their enemies. If people come into contact with these fish, they can become very ill or even die from the poison. Some may drown because of the terrible pain the poison causes.

Sharpshooter

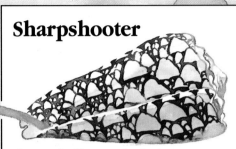

Cone shells attack their prey with a long tube tipped with teeth and loaded with poison. Large cone shells are hunted by shell collectors. Their poison can paralyze and kill.

A Deadly Handful

A blue-ringed octopus bites its prey, such as small crabs, and kills them with its deadly saliva. The octopus is only as big as an outstretched hand, but it is one of the deadliest creatures in the world. Many people who have picked it up have died.

A lionfish is one of the most poisonous fish in the sea. It swims slowly around coral reefs, showing off its bright, striped body to warn off predators. The poison lies in grooves in the spines on its back, and others near its head and tail.

28

A smaller member of the lionfish family is the scorpionfish. Its poison acts like the sting of a scorpion. From its markings and powerful poison, it is easy to see why this fish is called a zebrafish, firefish and even dragonfish.

Stone Dead

A stonefish may be the most poisonous fish of all. It lies very still on the sea bed, where its bumpy body blends in with the rocky background. Anyone who steps on a stonefish suffers great pain, and may die.

Jaws of Death

Some sharks have the strongest teeth of any animal. A great white shark's razor-sharp teeth can grow 3 ins (7.5 cm) long.

These vicious hunters attack and kill many swimmers every year. They can grow almost 26 ft (8 m) long and weigh over 3 tons.

Did You Know?

Sting rays have sharp spines on their tails which they use to stab and sting enemies that come too close. A person who is attacked by a sting ray may have trouble breathing. Some people have died.

All sea snakes are poisonous. One drop of poison from the beaked sea snake would be enough to kill five people. Fishermen die every year, bitten by snakes they have caught in their nets.

A swordfish will attack almost anything. Armed with a long, sharp "sword", it speeds through the water, stabbing and slashing shoals of small fish. Then it swallows its victims whole.

Many sea urchins have poisonous spines which, if trodden on, cause painful swellings. Some people eat the insides of sea urchins but the flesh can be poisonous and causes sickness.

Did You Know?

Shedding Shells

A female jonah crab sheds her shell before she mates. The male protects her while she waits for her new shell to harden. She carries her eggs around until they hatch into larvae.

Going Up in the World

Movements in the Earth's crust have pushed up great mountain ranges. Sea shell fossils in the Himalayas prove that these mountains were once under the sea, millions of years ago.

Animal in the Bath

Bath sponges are the remains of animals which live in the sea. After they are collected from the sea bed, the sponges are allowed to rot. Then they are washed and beaten until only the skeleton is left. Some sponges – not the ones that end up in the bath – grow up to 3 ft (1 m) across and weigh 110 lb (49 kg).

Back to the Sea

Life on Earth probably began in the sea. Land animals, including man, evolved from simple creatures that lived there hundreds of millions of years ago. Fossils show that some of those early animals still look the same today. The ancestors of whales lived on land. They returned to the sea 65 million years ago.

Top Speed

Tuna are streamlined for speed and are among the fastest fish in the sea. Their gill covers lie very close to their sides and their fins fold back into special grooves. Yellowfin tuna have reached speeds of 45 mph (72 km/h). When they smell, hear or see food, such as mackerel, herring, sardines, anchovies or flying fish, they can reach top speed in a second. Tuna have to swim to stay afloat. If they stop, they sink slowly towards the sea bed.

Blood Test

Sea plants and creatures are sometimes used in medicines to help human beings. Blood taken from horseshoe crabs is used to test drugs for poisons. The crabs are put back into the sea but many of them soon die.

A Mouthful of Plates

A baleen whale may have as many as 400 thin plates of baleen hanging down on either side of its top jaw. These plates, which are used to filter food out of the water, can grow up to 12 ft (4 m) long. They are very light and bendy, and have been used to make such things as ladies' corsets, fishing rods and the ribs of umbrellas.

Giant Floaters

Sunfish spend most of their lives swimming lazily on the surface of the water. They have no tails, and can grow up to 10 ft (3 m) long and weigh 1 ton. They feed mainly on jellyfish and are protected from their enemies by a layer of gristle under their skin.

Unwelcome Current

Every two to ten years, a warm current, called El Niño, flows past the coast of Peru, with disastrous effects on the local fishing catch. The warm water kills the plankton on which the fish, mainly anchovies, feed so the fish move away. The current is called El Niño, which means "the child" in Spanish, because it appears around Christmas.

Feathery Fans

Under the water, the colored tentacles of the peacock worm fan out to catch food. At low tide, only about 4 in (10 cm) of the worm's mud tube sticks out of the sand. The other end of the tube is attached to stones, often 14 in (35 cm) buried down in the sand.

Boring Piddock

A common piddock has two shells, covered with as many as 50 rows of spines. It bores into cliffs and rocks on the sea shore by twisting from side to side. The hole it drills may be up to 12 in (30 cm) deep.

Night Noises

Gurnards are very noisy fish. They make strange grunting and growling noises with their swim bladders. The sounds may help them to keep in touch with each other as they feed on the muddy sea bed. They may also help to keep other fish away from their eggs at spawning time.

On the Move

The map of the world is changing very, very slowly as the continents move on the Earth's crust. The size and shape of the oceans are also changing very, very slowly. The Pacific Ocean is growing smaller while the Atlantic Ocean is getting wider, by a few inches a year.

Pincer Punches

One species of crab protects itself by carrying a small sea anemone in each of its pincers. The anemone's stinging tentacles keep any predators away. The crab uses its front legs for feeding so that it does not have to let go of its protective weapon, the sea anemone.

On the Rocks!

Californian sea otters get the flesh out of clams and sea urchins by hammering them on a rock. The otter floats on its back, with a rock resting on its stomach. It holds a shell in its front paws, smashes it open and has a delicious feast.

Leaving a Mark

Weddell seals have a layer of fat under their skins to keep them warm. They are so well insulated against the freezing cold of the Antarctic Ocean that they can get too hot when the Sun shines. Then a seal's blood flows just under its skin to cool it down. The heat it gives off is enough to melt the snow under its body. When the seal moves away, it leaves a print on the ice.

Devil Fish

Manta rays flap slowly through the warm seas, like huge bats. Their giant "wings" are up to 21 ft (6.5 m) across, almost as big as a small, single-engined aircraft. Called the devil fish because it slowly swims around small boats, it is quite harmless, has no teeth and eats only plankton and shrimps.

Seaweed Shopping List

Agar, a gel extracted from certain seaweeds, is used to make all sorts of things, such as ice cream, pills, paint, beer, make-up creams, camera film and sewing thread. Fossils of tiny algae are used in toothpastes to make them rougher.

Index

j574.9
Swallow

First published in the United States of America.
in 1991 by The Mallard Press.

ISBN 0-7924-5524-X

Mallard Press and its accompanying design and logo are
trademarks of BDD Promotional Book Company, Inc.

Produced by Mandarin Offset.
Printed and bound in Hong Kong.

Edited and designed by Mitchell Beazley International Ltd.
Artists' House, 14-15 Manette Street, London W1V 5LB.

© Mitchell Beazley Publishers 1991
All rights reserved.

Typeset in Garamond ITC by Kerri Hinchon.
Reproduction by Mandarin Offset, Hong Kong.